MY theology

The Serendipity of
Life's Encounters

T0002334

Ann
Loades

The Serendipity of
Life's Encounters

Fortress Press

Minneapolis

THE SERENDIPITY OF LIFE'S ENCOUNTERS

Print ISBN: 978-1-5064-8445-7
eBook ISBN: 978-1-5064-8446-4

Cover design: Kristin Miller

Contents

Introduction

As my following narrative will explain, reflection on 'my theology' is only possible because I happened to be able to apply for an initial academic degree in Theology in the days when women (at last) were finally able to do so, although as what we might go on to earn our livings – unless as schoolteachers – was hardly on our horizons. It was certainly no part of our expectations that we might actually become fully-fledged members of a Department of Theology, let alone teach in a 'theological college' in which men engaged with their training for ordination. The staff of my secondary school included some remarkable teachers, and, when I discovered that it was possible to go to a university with a range of possible options, I plumped for Theology, probably in part because so far as I knew no one from my school had ever opted for it before.

Given the character of the degree (focussed on the Christian origins of the Western Church), I might never have discovered the philosophical dimensions of Theology, had it not been my very good fortune to have Alec Whitehouse as my personal Tutor. Alec had a rigorously scientific background, was a theologian who read the work of Austin Farrer as well as Karl Barth, and an excellent 'manager' in any academic institution in which he found himself. I am not, of course, in any sense a 'trained' philosopher. It was through one of Alec's connections that I was able to apply for a Graduate Teaching Fellowship at McMaster University, Hamilton, Ontario, opting for two courses: one on the texts of Plato, Aristotle and Augustine, the other on Medieval Philosophy. These were to prepare for my dissertation on Leibniz' *Theodicy*.

My instincts for survival were well developed in my first appointments back in Durham, in which I completed the doctorate which would enable me to move from the limitations of the role I filled as a 'college officer' – which, among other things, involved a great deal of 'pastoral' work with undergraduates – into something else. I may add that along with my instinct for survival, I was singularly blessed with the support of colleagues in the Department of Theology. I completed a sort of 'carpet-bag' of a doctorate, the most original parts of which were concerned with Kant's engagement with theodicy post-Leibniz, and the efforts made by S. T. Coleridge to transmit Kant's work into English-speaking theology and philosophy. Most non-scientists did not have doctorates, but it was essential for someone like myself (i.e. female) to be able to establish credibility as a potential academic in a competition for a job, in the unlikely event of one becoming available, which as it happened, it did. I was fortunate in that I joined the Durham Department when Theology was changing to allow for new developments in familiar areas – which became refreshingly unfamiliar – and enabled the eventual recognition of areas of considerable significance. These included, for example, theology and ethics, sociology and the study of 'religion', literature, spirituality, the 'arts' (broadly speaking), and whole swathes of ecclesiastical history, so I had many opportunities to learn from my colleagues as well as to endeavour to make myself useful in various ways. Being a 'statutory' woman in a university in my day had its uses, of course – opportunities abounded to learn all sorts of aspects of how an institution might run (or grind itself into problems).

As for the rest: I was such an oddity that I received invitations to give papers and present lectures on all sorts of topics, and said yes to them all, got cracking, thought hard, learned how to time 'presentations' to different kinds of audiences, learned to cope with airports, made life-long friends both in the UK and the USA, and, as it happened, was much graced by some outstanding candidates studying for doctorates, some of them now distinguished clergy, and some of those both ordained and outstanding academics who have pioneered new areas of Theology themselves. My first major 'break' came 'out of the blue', as it were, to receive the invitation to give the Scott Holland Lectures, for which I was provided with the topic 'Theology and the Significance of Gender'.

Given the accidents of finding good male friends and colleagues in so many places it was probably unlikely I would turn my back on the religious tradition in which I had grown up, and I found it fascinating to discover both how women had negotiated their lives in different cultural and historical circumstances, and what problems in particular had faced them, as well as trying to negotiate my own. And when life became difficult, as it certainly did, I tried to act on the maxim offered by one of my colleagues: 'Grow a thicker skin.' My approach to topics in Theology is no doubt idiosyncratic, but at least I do not think I sound or read like anyone else – of course, this is entirely by accident and never by design. Serendipity has its merits!

1

A theology of social concern learned from schooling

FOR ME, DISCOVERING theology came about by sheer accident. Its roots lay in my schooling, starting as early as my experiences at my very first school, in the 'nursery' part of a boarding school for children whose parents needed to find them somewhere safe from bombs and the threats of worse to come. We were 'evacuees', far too young to be away from the only person or people we knew, and hating it – in my case until I changed schools at age eleven. To begin with we were all boys and girls together, though the boys tended to disappear as soon as their fathers found somewhere else, out of a context in which boys might become 'sissies'. We all lost good friends that way.

The nursery part of school did have its interests, however. Around the room in which we were taught there was an illustrated alphabet frieze in colour: 'A' to 'Z', with appropriate fruit or birds or animals. I must have learned this very quickly because I remember being able to read my first, short sentence, 'The fox sat on the mat', and being able to picture the fox from the frieze, sitting on a mat in front of a good fire. Perhaps as a result I have always been fascinated by animals and the non-human world, and have never understood how anyone could be indifferent to the context in which we currently find ourselves – this world so full of variety, colour, and ingenious creatures with whom we share so much. Disastrous indifference in the case of formal theology has also been the case in the churches, so many of which were so entertainingly decorated with non-human creatures in the past.

I found solace in books, comics, magazines and whatever else I could discover to read. There were no books at home. The word 'book' meant something in print which was not a newspaper, and until I was old enough to trundle off to a library, I was very dependent on whatever came into the house – if anything. Holidays were a trial of a different kind – being looked after by the woman with whom my hard-working mother had found lodgings for us. Along with the other few children around I used to escape into the nearest park for as much a part of a day as was possible.

At my first school, there was an outstanding teacher, Mrs Matthews, who introduced us to just about everything. We learned to read aloud, which was essential to getting to grips with a text; and we learned a lot 'by heart'. Learning to use pen and ink was predictably a disaster – scratchy pens, ink wells and blotting paper, with (later) fountain pens only a little better. This was years before the invention or accessibility of biros, let alone the big fat variety which I could get a hold on that made it easier to write. Piano lessons, school singing sessions, and some beginners' dancing lessons triggered my intense enjoyment of the 'performing arts'. 'Art' was in short supply, apart from hours spent colouring 'doilies' with coloured pencils, but I loved the art lessons at my next school, in Oldham, Lancashire.

I managed to pass the entrance

examination to that school, which was two bus-rides away in each direction (but we had a hot meal in the middle of the day). One feature of the entrance examination was reading aloud from Johanna Spyri's *Heidi* (I even managed to pronounce the names of the goats!). Those of us beginning school in the new arrivals class had to take turns to read aloud from Scripture in morning assembly. We always had good teachers of history, and somewhere along the line I latched on to the importance of learning what had happened in Europe in the previous two centuries, appalling though it was. One consequence of this was that I have always been interested in 'context' when trying to understand 'theology'; that is, I need to know *why* a topic fascinates someone, *where* they came from, *what* was happening in their country.

In the main school, there was always a selection process for reading at a Carol Service, and there were competitions (which I never entered) at junior and senior level for prizes for reading aloud. If there is one skill

I learned which could be transferred to just about anywhere – including, eventually, giving lectures or papers, or reading a 'lesson', or delivering my own sermons – it was that of getting used to my own voice in a formal setting. This was invaluable. Some of the formal settings (cathedrals) in which I learned to read out loud were huge! The school had an interest in how we read, for if we were to progress beyond the age of eighteen it was likely that it would be helpful for us to shed our Lancashire accents in public, so we gradually learned to do so. Moreover, I had a 'star' for my first essay in Nature Study, an essay about 'The Mole', so I was beginning to learn to write short pieces as well.

My school was a 'direct grant' grammar school for girls, in the days when there were far fewer such places for girls than there were for boys. The uniform was hideous; track suits were unheard of, so we were turned out to play ball games (at which I was hopeless) in bitter weather wearing our indoor clothes. Our exit aired the classrooms. Unlike home they were at least warm, and in some places there were hot pipes on which we could gratefully sit, so we could thaw out during the next lesson. Back in class, I spent a lot of time reading ahead under cover of my desk.

Many of the teachers lived close to the school, and when retired were always invited back to school events, which gave me an initial glimpse of the importance of 'community' which had nothing to do with 'church'. We could have piano lessons, which I took right the way through school, becoming a fast 'sight reader', and learned to cope with nerves for in-school 'recitals' of what we had learned during a term. We had an outstanding teacher of music, Mr Noel Walton, brother of the orchestral composer Sir William, so we heard piano transcriptions of the latter's music on many occasions.

I hoped to study music beyond school, not least to have singing lessons, but succumbed both to discouragement ('You can't make a living from music!') and the sheer difficulty of finding teachers at university and in my first years of being a school teacher myself. So singing in choirs, when possible, became my 'practice', and experiencing music in churches and cathedrals generated in me a sense of 'transcendence' and indeed made worship possible. When I managed to take up dance lessons again (both 'classical' ballet, and 'Graham technique', learned on 'summer schools' which became holidays and where friendships grew), I found having done so much music and being able to sing a melody simply invaluable. This was also the case when I qualified to teach ballet. I was hopeless at teaching young children, and best with teenagers and with adults – not least adult beginners.

We also had an extraordinary person teaching Scripture: Miss G. P. Pestle, who had two brothers who had read Theology at University College, Durham ('The Castle') in preparation for ordination. Miss Pestle was strangely dressed, and taught in a way particular to herself, but somehow we learned that she was profoundly compassionate, not least to animals. I loved the 'First' Testament, which somehow was connected to my Jewish friends in school (these friends did not attend morning assembly, which, as it happened, was minimally 'Christian' so far as I recall). Shalmaneser, Tig-Lath Pileser (or 'Pul'), the Rabshakeh, and others all helped to focus my attention onto the map of the 'Middle East', and to the interplay of ancient empires. I was also fascinated by the Gospels, but apart from the maps of the Mediterranean and St Paul's supposed journeys, and therefore something about Greek and Roman history, I found little to enthral me in Pauline theology. Of course, no one ever suggested that St Paul was visiting churches founded by women.

When I and another student opted for 'A' level Scripture, Miss Pestle took the two of us under her wing. On one occasion she took us into Manchester to hear Trevor Huddleston CR, in the days of his successful book *Naught for your Comfort*, in a packed-out hall in the city. This gave me my first glimpse of 'political theology'. It was not until years later that I was able to visit South Africa for a conference there, at the invitation of John De Gruchy, and to learn a little of just how the struggle to dismantle apartheid had been endured, and the part that theologians had played in it. The Free Trade Hall in Manchester was home to the Hallé orchestra (conducted by Sir John Barbirolli, for one) and it was possible with cheap bus fares to pay a few shillings to sit up in a gallery alongside other school and university students, both to hear music 'live' and actually to see how it was performed. There were plays to see at the Library Theatre, and it was also possible to pay to stand at the back of the stalls or circle of both the two main theatres in town, hoping to be able to sneak into an unclaimed seat at the interval. I saw *West Side Story*, as well as Margot Fonteyn in *Firebird*, that way. There was also the John Rylands Library to study in during the day. Meeting there to find the company of other students became a priority once at university.

When I became sixteen, my father ceased to pay any contribution for my maintenance, so it looked as if I might have to leave school. I looked at various options, one of the most obvious being that of nursing, my mother's profession, at which she was outstandingly good, usually, of course, as with all too many others, working extra hours through most of her working life without 'overtime' pay.

I plucked up courage to approach my headmistress, saying that I had heard about university as a possibility, and that I wanted to do my 'A' levels. She took the opportunity to say, both to myself and to others, that it was advisable not to apply to certain universities, as we would not get in. The idea that the school might find out how to implement a programme which would give girls from a Lancashire grammar school a chance of applying to such places seemed not to have occurred to anyone, least of all to have been required by the Governing Body, so we picked up the message that the school was somewhat lacking in confidence in our abilities. This was not exactly helpful to 'first generation' applicants to university, then or now. My headmistress found me a Governing Body scholarship, however, which enabled me to stay at school for another two years. Nowadays my school raises money to fund many pupils all the way through their years there, since it is located in a seriously deprived post-industrial area.

I have no recollection of how I came to opt for Theology, with teaching Scripture in a school the only obvious possibility it would create for me, given a Dip. Ed. to follow graduation. There was no 'career' guidance, of course, either at school or later at university. This was my first experience of doing something simply because no one had done it before, which was to stand me in excellent stead, despite the wholly unexpected emotional cost of moving from one college to another, and then out of my second college to full-time work in the Department of Theology in Durham. I was not conscious at the time of deliberately making my choice of shifting a 'block', for myself or others. At school, one consequence of my choice was that I took 'A' level Latin 'solo', and learned at that point that I could learn a language if I spoke it, as we did a lot of work by speaking the texts. Virgil's *Aeneid IV* ('Dido and Aeneas') was fascinating, not least for the glimpses it gave me of Roman religion. We also tackled some Greek, though unsurprisingly without enthusiasm for Xenophon's military adventures in his *Anabasis*. Greek and Latin for Early Church History texts (including the development of the Creeds) were to become familiar as part of Honours Theology at Durham, though nothing could have prepared us for the very peculiar Greek of the New Testament.

The school also thought that 'academic' girls might be helped along by cookery lessons, in a new, purpose-built Domestic Science extension, probably suspecting that many of us came from homes where food and cooking could receive but little if any attention. Learning how to cook scones and sausage rolls was, of course, not much use in later life, so when we left most of us bumped up the sales of Katharine Whitehorn's admirable book, *Cooking in a Bedsitter*. One thing I was to learn later on was the importance of being able to offer and receive hospitality in the form of a meal for and with friends – integral to 'religious' practice, with or without a 'grace'.

Another feature of school that I remember was the annual collection made of clothing and gifts for an abysmally poor part of Manchester, one of the ways in which the habit of 'charitable' giving was instilled in us. Many girls knitted blankets from 'squares', but, since I had been introduced to knitting by being offered grey yarn with which to make what were supposed to be dishcloths (floor cloths more likely), I refused to contribute to blanket-making. In sheer desperation I had already learned to make my own clothes, so was able to make some sort of contribution.

In the days and years of rationing in Britain, there was a national distribution of some basic foods, which had the effect of largely eliminating many forms of 'rickets', still visible in the appearance of elderly women who lived near our school. We could never have anticipated the scandalously necessary 'food banks' current in the UK, now apparently just part of life for people seriously disadvantaged through no fault of their own. School made us conscious of the needs of others, and in time I learned that 'religions' characteristically were clear about the priority of various forms of 'hospitality', not least for 'strangers'. At some point I decided to go on my own to a church down the road – 'black' Church of England-style, as it then was – where I learned the language of the Book of Common Prayer and the King James Bible. Yet I am clear that the substance of my introduction to 'religion', and theology, in one way or other was given its foundation primarily via my schooling rather than 'church'.

2

University teachers outside as well as inside formal teaching

BEFORE THE ROBBINS Report,[1] the expansion
of university places, and the foundation of
new universities in the 1960s, applications
to university were made on a form supplied
by each institution as the result of someone
or other's suggestion. Mine obviously came
from Miss Pestle. Durham University was tiny,
more or less cohering around the peninsula
of the River Wear, with minimal lecture room
provision, and the requirement of much walking
to and fro, aiding the possibility of making
friends with students from other colleges,
themselves very small in number. There
might have been a room with a telephone for
'the Professor' in some departments, but not
even that for Theology, which was organised
from the study in the house of the Van Mildert

[1]   http://www.educationengland.org.uk/documents/
robbins/robbins1963.html

Canon Professor in the Cathedral College (Van Mildert was the bishop who had made possible the founding of Durham University).

As it happened, Theology had some extraordinary academic staff at the time I studied there. For in the decade 1940-1950, Arthur Michael Ramsey (then the Van Mildert Professor) had made three crucial appointments to reconstitute the department, and none of them members of the Church of England, despite the fact that the men reading Theology were all destined for ordination. My cohort of four women was of course ineligible for anything of the kind by virtue of being female. Ramsey himself had come from a Nonconformist tradition, and understood the importance of Theology as an ecumenical endeavour, not least after the horrors of the Second World War.

Two of the three men were to retire from Durham, and their very stability at the institution made possible their publications, which became of major importance. The first was C. Kingsley Barrett, a Methodist, who had begun his university life as a mathematician, before switching to Theology, and was profoundly influenced by E. C. Hoskyns' translation of Karl Barth's work on *Romans.* Kingsley also had a talent for making his scholarly work eminently intelligible, and in effect wrote theology 'systematically', following his father as a preacher travelling to Methodist chapels on a weekly basis, however small the congregations. He was also to provide sustained critical and constructive argument for Methodists against 'reunion' with the Church of England given its episcopal establishment – very wisely as it has turned out.

Ramsey's second appointment was Charles Cranfield, a 'classicist-turned-theologian', originally ordained as a Methodist. By 1942, Charles had volunteered as a military chaplain with combat units in Europe, and was later given responsibility for prisoners of war, inevitably meeting some of the theologians of the 'German Christians' movement. Becoming a 'Reformed' minister and another fine preacher, he was by far the most formidable New Testament exegete of his generation, given his familiarity with Patristic writers and further centuries of struggle with *Romans*. His major life-work was the development of his massive International Critical Commentary on *Romans* – as it were, an exegetical base for the reading of Barth's *Church Dogmatics* as that emerged into post-war Anglophone theological currency. Students came to realise that, from his war experience, Charles sustained an articulate political sensitivity, his collection of letters revealing his first to Churchill as an MP (13/9/1938) and his last to newspapers on the setting up of Guantanamo Bay prison, which placed those incarcerated there in a legal limbo beyond the reach of USA or International law, as of course had been the terrible fate of many in wartime.

Both Kingsley and Charles lectured to us, though we were somewhat overwhelmed by Charles' learning as he worked through the writing of his ICC commentary. We simply did not have the language skills to cope, nor the training in using biblical commentaries required. We had to find commentaries on the English translations and then revert to our lecture notes. We learned, however, that theology could be of political importance.

Looking back on the degree, far too much was left to us in a whole range of areas to find out for ourselves, without having the library or other resources – including classes and seminars – we needed, which did nothing to either enable or encourage many of us to continue with whole areas of Theology. Hardly anyone ever received 'first'-class marks for anything whatsoever; it simply was not 'policy' to award them, which was baffling, and did nothing to lead us to suppose we could do really well. This is characteristic of much university education in the past, though mercifully not of the present. 'Grade inflation' was much needed, with students now examined on what they have been taught, by a variety of methods, and above all, able to write excellent dissertations on subjects they themselves choose. We were grateful and impressed to find that both Kingsley and Charles become Fellows of the British Academy (the Academy's 'Biographical Memoirs of the Fellows' are available to read on the internet).

Each member of the academic staff had a tutorial group, the members of which had to walk through Durham to their tutor's respective homes. One-by-one teaching was of course a godsend. Each of us was given at least an hour a week in which we staggered through reading an essay out loud, inevitably patch-worked from whatever we could find in libraries, and hopelessly inadequate by today's standards, minus footnotes or bibliography, and no real demonstration of how to tackle essay-writing. On the other hand, we did learn to respond to interruptions from our tutor as we attempted to read out what we had learned as the result of our scavenging in the library, and learned to think differently about all kind of topics. Our tutor's job was basically to see to it that we had enough material in some form or another (apart from scrawled lecture notes) to get through exam papers. The blessing of such an arrangement was that the academic staff took a serious interest in us, generous with many extra hours of 'face-time'. They introduced us to excellent coffee, and some of them became life-long friends who did whatever they could to sustain us through the difficulties we might face. We also came to be invited by others of the academic staff to their homes for meals, meeting their families, which was another godsend to many of us.

In my particular case, I found myself in the tutorial group of W. A. Whitehouse, 'Alec' – the third non-Anglican Ramsey had introduced to the staff. As I was to discover, Alec had begun to learn German at school, and in 1936, as a twenty-one-year-old, graduated from Cambridge in the Mathematical Tripos. He moved to Mansfield College, Oxford, to study Theology in preparation for entering the Congregational ministry, and there was able to appreciate Austin Farrer's admirable sermons as Chaplain and Fellow of Trinity College, whilst writing a thesis in Philosophical Theology which earned him a B. Litt. degree. In his turn he was to develop into a notable preacher, not least for BBC broadcast services.

From his earliest days at Mansfield, Alec became personally acquainted with members of the German Church struggle, both on a visit to Germany in 1938, and with refugee ministers in Oxford, fully alert to the contribution of Barth in supporting resistance to the 'German Christians' movement. Unsurprisingly, he had little time in later life for those who suffered from 'softening of the bones, especially of the spine'. This served him well in the course of later responsibilities in the new University of Kent, to which he was to move in 1965 as Master of Eliot College, and the university's first Professor of Theology. This was in good time to withstand the student 'troubles' of 1968, which in the longer term precipitated much more government attention to universities than had ever been the case in the past, with increasing pressure to opt for 'utilitarian' subject areas.

In 1946 he visited Germany as the representative of the English Free Churches, the fruit of the efforts made by Bishop G. K. A. Bell of Chichester, and then, appointed to Durham, he shared a course in Doctrine for ordinands with A. M. Ramsey until the latter departed for brief occupancy of the Regius Chair in Cambridge. Charles Cranfield and he got on particularly well.

Alec taught two courses, and, despite the availability of his 'Reformation Theology', I managed to graduate and remain almost completely ignorant of the theology of that era, apart from later reading Luther's incomparable sermons. The other course Alec taught, on 'Philosophy and the Christian Religion: Anselm, Aquinas, Hume and Kant', all requiring the reading of texts, was the one which engaged me the most.[2] This was especially the case with Anselm's *Proslogion*, given the superb way in which he integrated prayer with argument in that

---

[2] Ed. Ann Loades, W. A. Whitehouse, *The Authority of Grace: Essays in Response to Karl Barth* (Edinburgh: T & T Clark, 1981) includes examples of a whole range of his different styles of 'theology'.

work, and then both his *Meditation on Human Redemption* and other prayers. Somehow or other, I also took to Kant's work, not least his *Critique of Judgment.* This led me into Kant's least-read essays of the 1790's, prompted by some remarks of Professor Donald MacKinnon FBA, whom I first met at conferences of the Society for the Study of Theology.

I also seized the opportunity to attend lectures in the Philosophy department given by Dr Wolfgang von Leyden. Alec's personal research interests were in the possible relationship of science and theology, not least as a participant in the conversations taking place in Germany. He attended the annual meetings of the Societas Ethica[3] (for years, he was the sole British attendee), which he was eventually to encourage me to join. Since it met in a variety of European locations, that introduced me to mainland Europe and prompted and sustained my developing interests in theology-and-ethics as well as theology-and-politics.

[3] European Society for Research in Ethics.

Having managed to cope with a Dip. Ed. course, and finding myself a job in a girls' grammar school in the south of England, it was not long before I could see that I was unlikely to survive teaching 'Scripture' long term. I found that if I could manage to teach the fourth Gospel in the last teaching slot on a Friday afternoon I could probably cope with just about anything, but not indefinitely. One unexpected result was that I learned more about that Gospel than when I had taken my degree.

As it so happened, Alec had been approached by a representative of the newly-founded Department of Religion at McMaster University, Hamilton, Ontario, which had a graduate teaching fellowship to offer. This involved taking two graduate courses, writing a dissertation, and teaching seminars for first year students. A 'modular' MA was unheard of in the UK, let alone the involvement of graduate students in undergraduate teaching. Moreover, it was almost impossible to obtain funding for further study in the UK at that time, so I was delighted to be one of a group of UK graduates who found themselves in Canada for a year (1963–64, followed by an MA in 1965). It gave me my first experience of teaching both male and female undergraduates; for example, reading with them Plato's *Republic* which was new to me. I also had my own essays for my modules to struggle with, after three years of doing nothing of the kind, with virtually no secondary resources for 'Humanities' in the McMaster library at that time, and I was also trying to focus on my dissertation.

I was, however, fortunate indeed to have arrived just a couple of years after the Department of Religion had been founded by George P. Grant, who was from a most distinguished family of academics and politicians. At my first meeting with him he had asked me what I had studied in Durham, and, on being informed, simply remarked that if he had to choose between Semitic religion and Augustine, 'Semitic religion could go'. I did not attempt to explain or commend to him my love of the Book of Isaiah from my days of struggling with the Hebrew text thereof as an undergraduate. (Isaiah was later the subject of two splendid contrasting books by another friend, Professor J. F. A. Sawyer, of the University of Newcastle on Tyne.)[4]

The course I was supporting was for first-year students, gathered to hear George as he prowled the lecture area, minus notes of any kind, giving the most enthralling undergraduate lectures that I have ever had the privilege to hear and observe. We did not know that he was already writing *Lament for a Nation* (1965), but at some point or other he introduced me to Leo Strauss's *Persecution and the Art of Writing*, then to the volumes of Eric Voegelin's *The New Science of Politics* volumes, and some of the texts of Simone Weil. These were resources for theology of which I had never even heard, quite apart from my introduction to the work of those

---

[4] John F. A. Sawyer, *The Fifth Gospel* (Cambridge: Cambridge University Press, 1996); *Isaiah Through the Centuries* (Hoboken NJ/Chichester: Wiley Blackwell, 2018), a superb example of the new movement in 'reception exegesis' which he has helped to establish, and drawing on websites/the 'Arts' and his own expertise in Rabbinic literature.

who, like Dr von Leyden, had fled for their lives from Germany.

I re-learned enough French and Latin so that I could read G. W. Leibniz's *Theodicy* (including his 'De Causa Dei'), which was to be the subject of my dissertation, and worked at one of my two modules on Medieval Philosophy and Theology, which fed into the thought-world of Leibniz in addition to learning something of his other extraordinary achievements. Trips to Göttingen followed years later. Coping with Leibniz's extraordinary text (analysing his case for the divine calculation of world-making) was a formidable task for an MA dissertation. It was, of course, Alec's suggestion that I tackled it, not least because Austin Farrer had written the introduction to the new translation by E. M. Huggard (1952). Fortunately, I had learned to type whilst working one summer vacation in the office of Kellogg's Cornflakes in Manchester, so at least I had a useful 'keyboard skill' for my subsequent writing. Ian Ramsey (then in Oxford, later Bishop of Durham) examined my dissertation and later roped me into his

'Christian philosophers' group, which in later years eventually developed into the Society for the Study of Philosophy of Religion.

I had the option to move from McMaster to continue at Chicago, but Alec had supported me for a job as what was then called 'Resident Tutor' at my former Durham college, and I opted for that, intending to study for a doctorate with Alec. I had learned in Canada that if I was going to stay in Higher Education I would need a further degree, though I was to find on return to the UK that this was still comparatively rare, except in the sciences. Also on my return, however, I found that Alec was leaving for Kent. In any event, I was so overwhelmed with work that it took considerable time to begin to sort out a doctorate, which was then possible as an unsupervised member of staff with an 'adviser'. I had my own tutorial group in the Theology department, with no guidance as to what was expected of me, so blundered along as best I could on the basis of my earlier recollections and teaching experience. Eventually I was able to secure a small study in what became departmental premises, where I could work on my own and make friends with some crucially-important members of recently appointed staff.

At college, we were overwhelmed with applications from the recently-established Universities' Council arrangements for admissions. We managed with record cards for each candidate, and lists for the offers to be made to fill the quotas for each subject area, centrally allocated by the university. We interviewed all candidates, many of whom were benefitting from comprehensive school education, having been deemed 'failures' at 11+, and via telephone made contacts all over the university to agree decisions about whom was to be made an offer. That way, I learned something about what was of interest in other academic subject areas, and who was teaching what. We had to look up 'A' level results in the summer, as published by the various examining boards, by trundling down to a university office, there to encounter good colleagues from across the other colleges. So I learned how to crack problems in administration, minus computers and other such aids. By the time students sent in passport-sized photographs and arrived for their degree courses, I knew their faces, names and backgrounds, and a good deal about the schools they had attended. The ignorance about one's students nowadays – required by 'Data Protection' – was not then an issue.

3

The limitations of any 'systematic' theology; theodicy and abuse

ANOTHER TASK FACING me in my new role at my old Durham college was to sort out the shambles of its library, since the Governing Body was intending to put some money into it – not before time. Equipped with a Dewey 'short title' catalogue I plunged in, and, in a window box, found a notice signed by H. F. M. Prescott (a former Vice-Principal), of whom no other trace remained in either college or university it seemed. I knew just enough to appreciate the fact that she had written at least one outstanding book, the historical novel *The Man on a Donkey,* and found that she was also a Durham D.Litt. I bought and read her books (and put copies into the library). Her work prompted my realisation that literature could be of the first importance as a source for theology and philosophy.[5] I also realised that the elaborate philosophical theology of Leibniz was hardly a source of illumination for those facing their death on the *Pilgrimage of Grace*, the topic of her novel.

I was later to be exceptionally fortunate in developing life-long friendships with some superb graduate students who developed the interplay between 'Theology and Literature', and who kept me alert to the development of this whole new academic field which they made their own. Helen Waddell and Dorothy L. Sayers also had Durham D.Litt. degrees, I discovered, so I read everything I could lay my hands on of their work too; both contributed to Theology in distinctive ways. On occasion, it was possible to tie two books together for undergraduate attention, such as Iris Murdoch's *The Sovereignty of Good* and *Henry and Cato*, the one illuminating the other. I also

[5] Four Durham academics (three of them former students at various levels) were to develop 'Theology and the Arts'. See Ann Loades, 'Some SEC Theologians and the Arts', *Scottish Episcopal Church Institute Journal* (online), 5:2, (2021) 75-88.

began to look out for 'women in theology', for example adding to those I wrote about figures as diverse as Margery Kempe, Mary Wollstonecraft, Josephine Butler, Elizabeth Cady Stanton, Evelyn Underhill and Simone Weil.

I found ways of learning enough German to enable me to beaver away at Immanuel Kant's work, stretching through to the 1790s, and I was working my way into a thesis about 'theodicy' – meaning 'the vindication of God' regarding the question of why God permits the manifestation of evil – post-Leibniz, as the notion of the 'fixity of species' was giving way to those of 'transformism' and 'evolution'.

I also realised in time that I had clearly stayed at my first college too long if I was to make progress in university life. I was very fortunate in having become fast friends with John Rogerson in the Theology Department. John had emerged with Russian from the Joint Services School for Linguists during National Service with the RAF, and was appointed to Durham in 1964. He was ordained there and proved to be another fine preacher (minus notes!). He was a pioneer in recognising the significance of new disciplines such as sociology, anthropology and literary criticism for 'First Testament' Studies, and later moved to Sheffield as Professor, with his work recognised by the award of Honorary Doctorates from Jena and Freiburg.

Having learned on National Service how to crack a language, he taught himself German and was also a reader of Kant (and just about everything else, it seemed). He read my drafts as my unofficial 'adviser'. He provided a superb example of how to get through administration in order to free oneself up for writing, and supported me through the completion of a doctorate, which was just in time for me to apply for a full-time lectureship in Theology. In transition to that job I had found the nerve to request the Vice-Chancellor to take me off the relevant appointing committee so that I could apply for a post out of my first college into the same job in Durham's first 'mixed' college, to which I was appointed. There, the paperwork for the overwhelming rate of undergraduate applications was managed by secretarial staff, though I also had to get a college library on to the shelves from scratch.

As it so happened, I was able to apply for a full-time appointment in the university's Theology department after just two years when another member of the department retired. I was fortunate to have Dr P. J. Fitzpatrick (a brilliant member of the Philosophy department) on the committee, since my doctorate had not by then been examined. He read it, backed its quality, and made my appointment possible, despite the fact that I was certainly not the choice in 'Systematic Theology' that Stephen Sykes had wanted. Stephen had been appointed as Van Mildert Professor in 1974, and rightly had his sights set on transforming the teaching of Christian Theology for the undergraduates. He soon set up a Tübingen-Durham MA involving Ingolf Dalferth, which brought us students from Germany, some of whom stayed with us for their doctorates.

Systematic Theology was a relatively

new category in UK Theology at the time (for instance, 'Dogmatic Theology' was T. F. Torrance's 'Barthian' preference in Edinburgh), and, as Van Mildert canon professors came and went, the label changed to 'Contemporary Theology' (i.e. Christian theology in its contemporary setting).

Notoriously 'unsystematic' in my interests, I have long been astonished at the range of Theology wholly ignored by 'systematic theologians', although not in Stephen's case. Having come from a very privileged educational route, he stayed at Durham for a decade, during which time we became good friends and colleagues. I was also fortunate in that Professor Donald MacKinnon did a stint as external examiner for undergraduate degrees, and approved of what I had managed to teach in 'Philosophy and the Christian Religion', which both gave me some confidence and secured Stephen's support. Stephen was then making his case for the 'integrity' of Anglicanism, and, without a doctorate himself, became a superb supervisor of graduate students in what would now be called 'Anglican Studies', as well as representing Anglicanism internationally. Much of what I know about Anglicanism I learned primarily from him.

Shortly after my joining the department full time, Stephen was able to make an appointment of an entirely new kind of theologian, Richard H. Roberts. Richard emerged from a tough upbringing in home and grammar school via the first cohort of graduates from the programme in Religious Studies developed by Ninian Smart at the new University of Lancaster. He had then undertaken an MA in Cambridge, a doctorate in Edinburgh, and had studied in Tübingen. His particular strengths lay in his engagement with European Theology and Philosophy. Despite profound differences between them, he and Stephen developed a lecture and seminar programme which for its resources drew from across any and every Christian tradition, and was unique in its time.

There were of course other members of the department with strong international connections, and these were enhanced by the integration of St Cuthbert's Roman Catholic Seminary (Ushaw College) into the university in 1968. Staff and students from Ushaw (including some from religious orders) took degrees supervised by members of the department and shared teaching and academic life more generally, with warm friendships soon in place. It was one of the best times in the department for me personally, and, without making a deliberate policy of it, it was during this time that I became aware of the 'Calendar of Saints' insofar as such an emphasis flourished in the Church of England, and of the doctrines and traditions about Mary the Mother of Jesus and of women saints, and the saints more generally.[6]

My interest in theodicy continued, in part because I accepted invitations to lecture which provoked me into thinking about

[6] Ann Loades, *Grace is not Faceless: Reflections on Mary* (London: DLT, 2021). For my recent and forthcoming publications I continue to be deeply indebted to Professor Stephen Burns, University of Divinity, Melbourne, who, with Natalie Watson (Publishing Director of Sacristy Press) and both former Durham postgraduate students, edited a Festschrift for me. See note 9.

matters that required attention. For instance, I responded to an invitation to address the Church of England Hospital Chaplains' Fellowship on 'Death and Disvalue: sick children, their families and those who care for them'. This conference opened my eyes to the work of such specialisms, not least that of those who worked in Paediatric Departments in hospitals, and the most memorable address was from Dr Jane Goodall, then Consultant Paediatrician at City General Hospital, Stoke-on-Trent, about what happens when treatment ends and a child dies.[7]

For my reflections on that occasion I included some of the work of an 'Alice Grey'. I am not sure how I discovered that this was the very distinguished historian Margaret Spufford FBA, who, apart from her professional work, wrote the book *Celebration*, about the problem of pain and the experience of having a beloved daughter endure a genetically-caused disease with medical intervention, before dying aged twenty-two. I was able to include extracts from

[7] See the papers printed in *Hospital Chaplain,* December 1985, No. 93.

that book, and Margaret's journals containing some of her and her daughter's unpublished reflections, in a book of 'spiritual classics'.[8]

By this time, I had seriously taken on board something I had learned from Kant, which was that speculative theodicy of a Leibnizian mode did not begin to touch the tragedies which faced people in reality. For Kant had seen the point of the book of 'Job' – that God was the 'divine judge' of how we addressed ourselves to what we encountered in life, good or bad.[9] I also spotted that Austin Farrer's chapter, 'Griefs and Consolations', in his *Love Almighty and Ills Unlimited*, was very likely his response to his friend C. S. Lewis' *A Grief Observed* about the death of his beloved wife, Joy. The problem then was to make 'salvation'

[8] Ann Loades, *Spiritual Classics from the Late Twentieth Century* (London: Church House Publishing, 1995), 68-103, which also includes work by Helen Oppenheimer, Janet Martin Soskice, Cardinal Carlo-Maria Martini, Jacques Pohier and Kenneth Leech.

[9] See Elizabeth C. Galbraith, 'Kant, Job's comforters and Adolf Eichmann' in eds. Natalie Watson and Stephen Burns, *Exchanges of Grace: Essays in Honour of Ann Loades* (London: SCM, 2008) 155-164.

credible in a world in which God, as it were, allowed creatures of all levels of complexity principally to make themselves, even though with the promise or at least hope of blessing and ultimate 'rescue' given.

A paper on Farrer exploring him as 'preacher of divine saving judgment' was the first paper I gave at the second international conference on his theology and philosophy. The first of these had been organised by Brian Hebblethwaite (Cambridge) with two other colleagues, and the second one was in Princeton. Both that conference and the subsequent series were mostly focussed on Farrer's philosophy, so although I had no idea of what I was doing, apart from getting a much-needed paper at an international conference onto my record, mine introduced a different perspective on Farrer. For illustration, I drew on Rosemary and Victor Zorza's *A Way to Die*, which was about the death of their twenty-five year-old daughter (a book significant for the development of the 'hospice' movement), and Rolf Hochhuth's *A German Love Story*, which was about the fate of a Polish prisoner of war released for work on a German farm.

That was my only trip to Princeton, but over the years I much enjoyed lecturing and teaching in a whole variety of institutions in the USA, some of them the result of making contacts at future Farrer conferences both in the USA and the UK, and avoiding all but a few of the exhausting meetings of the American Academy of Religion. Colleges in the USA included some outstanding undergraduate teachers who did a great deal of research during vacations, as had been the tradition in the UK. The assumption of people in UK universities that college teachers did not do research because they were not supervising graduates was clearly nonsense. The focus of my attention away from 'theodicy' but into another troublesome area was about to change with a letter which arrived from the Scott Holland Trust.

4

Prejudice and feminist theology in the university

THE LETTER FROM the Scott Holland Trust contained an invitation (certainly not to be declined) to give some lectures on 'Theology and the Significance of Gender' – in those days, as it were, this was code for 'being female/feminine'.[10] The focus of the lectures was to be 'the religion of the Incarnation in its bearing on the social and economic life of man.'

So far as I know, I remain the only member of the Durham Department ever to be invited to deliver the Scott Holland Lectures. I could give them anywhere in the UK and, when I shared the exciting news with my friend Professor John Sawyer in Newcastle, where I had previously

[10] The 'Holland lectureship' had been founded in 1920 to perpetuate the memory and influence of Henry Scott Holland who had concluded his career as Regius Professor of Divinity in the University of Oxford.

given seminar papers, he invited me to give them as lunchtime Public Lectures there. The first was chaired by the then Chairman of the Trust, Bishop Kenneth Woollcombe, and the last by John himself.

I needed to leave Durham to be free to find out what on earth should be covered by the topic given to me. With the help of Professor Basil Mitchell (Oxford), I found someone to replace my teaching, and enough funding to travel and stay with Canon and Mrs John Fenton in Christ Church, Oxford. John had been Principal of St Chad's College, Durham, and Linda had taught our first year students their introductory New Testament Greek course. John had also provided my first opportunities to preach in St. Chad's Chapel, and I had gradually absorbed liturgy there, though little did I appreciate it at the time. Quite by accident, in Oxford I was also introduced to the Benedictines of St Benet's Hall, who were remarkably generous with hospitality both in Chapel and for dinners.

I was back in Durham for the term in which I was to give the lectures, and wrote them week by week. Richard Roberts very kindly accompanied me on my five trips to Newcastle, and sat through the lectures to an audience which grew, and which I gratefully came to appreciate for their interest and enthusiasm. The paperback which emerged from the lectures, *Searching for Lost Coins,* was the first monograph on 'feminist' theology to emerge from a UK university-based theologian, and from there I was launched into writing and lecturing in the area, bearing in mind the stimulus of post-Christian feminism.

While I then put together a 'Reader' in Feminist Theology,[11] Dr Ursula King (first in Leeds and later as Professor in Theology and Religious Studies in the University of Bristol) published on 'Third World' feminist theology. Both of us remained practicing members of our respective churches, she as a Roman Catholic, and myself as an Anglican. From the perspective of some feminists, of course, those who stayed within the Christian tradition

[11]   Ed. Ann Loades, *Feminist Theology: A Reader* (London: SPCK and Louisville: WJKP, 1990).

were seen as something of a nuisance – in two senses. On the one hand, we had not opened ourselves to the full force of the critique of such tradition to precipitate ourselves out of it. On the other, we were going to be a source of irritation to those who simply had not taken the measure of the inadequacies of those ecclesial institutions which embodied the long Christian tradition which deemed women to be inferior, and therefore subordinate, to men.[12] Although, strictly speaking, the issue of the ordination of women in the Church of England was not a matter for concern within the Durham Department of Theology, unfortunately it certainly affected working relationships between men in the department in quite unpredictable ways, quite apart from the expectations – or lack of them – some of them had of their women students.

It was inevitable that I became a 'statutory

[12] My one paper on pioneer Mary Daly: 'Beyond the Father: An Introduction to Mary Daly's View of Christian Tradition' in eds. Andrew Linzey and Peter Wexley, *Fundamentalism and Tolerance: An Agenda for Theology and Society* (London: Bellow, 1991), 113-27.

woman' in Durham; that is, I became required for a number of committees, from which I gained considerable insight into how the university worked as Vice-Chancellors changed. I also learnt a very great deal from being a member of a Civil Service Selection Board for Administrative Appointments between 1985 and 1993. The Civil Service had just abandoned assessment for entry via essay writing, which, interesting though the reports on candidates were, was a slow way of proceeding. New methods of assessment produced information much faster, and opened up competition for entry from those who had not spent their university years writing essays at speed on a very wide range of topics. Candidates were also assessed on how they participated in committees as a member and as chair of a committee, and whether they were able or not to write a 'brief' for a 'senior' at short notice, as well as being interviewed by a panel of assessors.

In addition, being an 'external' for other university institutions revealed to me that some places at least were expecting competitors for a job to be able to 'present' a topic within strict time limits, so there was plenty to feed back to the Theology Department at Durham, not least when I was plummeted (without discussion) into the role of Chairing the Board of Studies (1989-1991). This I would not have survived had it not been that Alan Ford (ex-Irish Foreign Service) had joined the department (he later became Professor of Theology at the University of Nottingham) and was roped in as Secretary of the Board, equally focussed on making necessary changes. Fortunately, we had also appointed Dr Carol Harrison to a lectureship (*en route*, as it were, to the Lady Margaret Professorship in Oxford and an FBA) so there was one other woman teaching Theology. It proved virtually impossible to find other female candidates for lectureships in Theology, not least because of the male excuse that 'We already have another woman in the department'. The situation has improved only to a limited extent to the present time, even with a significant increase of women in postgraduate work. Other subject departments, such as Philosophy, have a different story to tell.

At that time, introductory courses for such roles as chairing a department were barely on the horizon, so I asked a friend of mine from Business Studies about 'chairing', and we worked through a document which enlightened me – not that it prepared me for the obstructive behaviour of some of our colleagues when it actually came to implementing changes that had already been agreed, especially those relating to syllabus revision. Some of the anger and emotion which surfaced probably stemmed from the discussions taking place at that time in some churches about the possible ordination of women, as well as the sheer oddity of having a woman chairing meetings and reorganising whatever needed doing.

Having been taught by Nonconformists, who were familiar with women preaching and ministering in congregations, and having learned the biblical understanding of 'apostle' as having to do with witness to the 'resurrection' of Christ, and even of Mary of Magdala as 'apostle to the apostles' (from John 21) in post-biblical tradition, I had not taken the measure of the problems I might face. With friends who had moved from being 'deaconness' to 'deacon' to 'priest' – including one on the staff of the Cathedral – and women appointed as canons yet to come, I was not prepared for the furore of 1994, when the Church of England ordained women as priests for the first time. I recall, however, that Durham Cathedral was packed for the first Eucharist celebrated by the Revd Margaret Parker, the congregation including men who had brought their little daughters to be present so that they could be reminded that they had been there that day. Also present was a large group of Roman Catholic women, professionally qualified in many fields.

The newspaper report of a clergyman in Bristol having said 'Burn the bloody bitches/ witches'(reports varied) made it clear to me that if I pursued a possible vocation for ordination I would find the Durham

Department uncomfortable, to put it mildly. Later experiences on the Church of England's House of Bishops working party on Women in the Episcopate made me profoundly thankful that I could walk away from ordination without qualms.[13] I had no sooner finished chairing the department than I accepted the invitation to edit the journal *Theology*, despite being informed that SPCK 'had really wanted X, but he was too busy'. An interesting stint in this role from 1991 to 1997 introduced me to ranges of approaches to Theology entirely new to me, and, much to my surprise, gained me an entry in *Who's Who*.

Having put my head over the parapet, so to speak, I found myself with other invitations. First of all, I accepted a request to address the first national conference for Christian Survivors of Sexual Abuse, in York in 1993 – a gathering of women who had been abused in one way another by clergy from any and all ecclesial groups. At that stage of opening-up

[13] Ann Loades, 'Women in the Episcopate?', *Anvil: An Anglican Evangelical Journal of Theology and Mission*, 21 (2004), 113-119.

'abuse' for public acknowledgement it was clearly difficult to know how those attending the conference were ever going to be able to get their voices heard in their churches.

I was next invited to deliver the John Coffin Memorial Lecture in the University of London Senate House in 1994, and was given the topic 'Thinking about Child Sexual Abuse'. It seems that I was the first academic theologian to take on this agenda, and as a topic it was baffling and offensive to some of my departmental colleagues, and to clergy I was when invited to address them. 'In my village, a virgin was a girl who could run faster than her father,' was one unforgettable comment. Given that the lecture topic was specified, was a mark of public concern, and that it was published, I remain both baffled and irritated by those who continue at the present time to claim that 'no one even thought about abuse' (of children or anyone else) until very recently, to which one can only reply: 'Who did not know, and why did they not know until now?'[14]

Much to my personal shame, however, it has taken me years to even notice that very few theologians, whether feminist or non-feminist, have had 'children' in their sights, despite the work done years ago by the Revd Jeff Astley and the North of England Institute for Christian Education on the importance of the religious education of children (and adults too for that matter).[15] I am hoping that, having realised the normal ecclesial deficit of attention to children once past the 'buggy-morning' stage of hospitality available in churches, I have recently made one small and hopefully constructive proposal about how to engage them in worship. If there is attention given to children there, it might become possible to pay attention to them in

[14] Ann Loades, 'The Revelation of Abuse: Some Personal Reflections', *Scottish Episcopal Institute Journal* (online) 5: (2021) 17-30, on more than the abuse of children.
[15] See for example Revd Professor Dr Jeff Astley, 'Researching the field of Christian education: reflections on an English experiment', in ed. Brian Gates, *Insider and Outsider Perspectives on Religious Education in England*, (Tübingen: Mohr-Siebek, 2016) 327-348.

all aspects of their lives, and anything but as 'objects' of abuse.[16]

The year 1995, at which time there was still only one female professor in any Durham department, happened to be the centenary of the year in which the university had renegotiated its conditions for the award of degrees, to permit women to graduate in any faculty except Divinity (a situation which had obviously changed). Previous Vice-Chancellors had managed to appoint more women in a range of departments, but the incumbent Vice-Chancellor, Evelyn Ebsworth, took this opportunity to celebrate the centenary by having a special ceremony for the award of higher Degrees to eminent women. I proposed philosopher Mary Midgley (Newcastle), from whose books and acquaintance I had learned so much over the years, and Barbara Reynolds, the Dante expert and writer/editor on the work

[16] Ann Loades, 'Children and Liturgy' in eds. Gordon Jeanes and Bridget Nichols, *Lively Oracles of God: Perspectives on the Bible and Liturgy*, (Collegeville, MN: Liturgical Press, 2002) in press.

of Dorothy L. Sayers, both for D.Litt. degrees. The latter had invited me to meetings of the Sayers Society and I had invited her back to Durham for Sayers-related occasions. I myself was awarded the first 'personal' chair in the history of the university, soon to be followed by many others in a range of departments. This did not enhance my popularity with some members of my department, one of whom took it upon himself to email his advice about 'how to be a professor', which of course I could work out for myself as my priorities were shifting yet again. Getting out of the department, I enjoyed myself accepting invitations to universities in Europe, Australia and South Africa, sometimes to lecture or to participate in conferences, and sometimes to act as an examiner or as 'external assessor' for grants or promotions.

Another 'breakthrough' was becoming a panel convenor for Philosophy, Theology/ Religious Studies and Law' (i.e. post-graduate awards) for the newly constituted Arts and Humanities Research Board/

Council (AHRB/C), and thus, with other panel convenors a member of its Postgraduate Committee. I recall the occasion on which, for the first time in my life, I walked into a meeting of academic staff fifty per cent of whom were women. Whoever had set up the AHRB/C had clearly thought carefully about how to represent the changes that had taken place in 'Higher Education'. Chairing the panel, and working with colleagues across our group of disciplines for several years, provided me with a clear view of what were already, around the turn of the millennium, indications of which strands in Theology and Religious Studies were flourishing and which were not. The result was that if certain areas were to survive, appointments would have to be made of academics from outside the UK. In the light of what I had discovered, when President of the Society for the Study of Theology in 2005-06 I did my best to stir my colleagues into concern about the future of their areas of discipline in Theology and Religious Studies, and much has happened since – at last – to stir people out of what was then complacency about the future of the whole subject area.[17]

The years in which I was much interested in the AHRB/C included the morning when, to my utter astonishment, I opened in my post a letter which invited me to indicate on an enclosed form my willingness (or not) to accept a CBE. As I was to learn, the only previous such award 'for services to Theology' had been to the New Testament Scholar, C. F. D. Moule. I do not know who made the proposal for my award, but suspect it was the Vice-Chancellor, Evelyn Ebsworth, who had taken the initiative to have me proposed for a personal chair. So, in 2001, with help from friends, two great parties followed – one in Durham, and one in London.

In addition, together with a colleague from Classics, Dr David Hunt, I became the first of two lay members of Durham Cathedral Chapter (2001-2007), as the result of the Church

[17] Ann Loades, 'A wake-up call', *Theology*, 123:2020, 124-128, addressed to the Church of England as much as to the academic community, which now (at last) has a website; https://trs.ac.uk.

of England's Synod seeing the point of having lay members of cathedral congregations on their Governing Body. In my case, one of my tasks continued to be sorting out a library of German Theology donated to the Cathedral (subsequently this has been relocated into the University). That particular activity was a kind of education in itself! With another 'reform' in progress in 2021-22, Durham Cathedral life continues to flourish with its Chapter of 'team players', employees and volunteers. In 2007, I became a Lay Canon at a ceremony conducted by Bishop N. T. Wright, and in 2008 a Lay Canon Emerita.[18]

[18] Ann Loades, 'Think about Cathedrals: discover ecclesiology', *Modern Believing*, 61:3, 2020, 252-258.

5

The arts and new moves in Theology

THERE WAS ONE more shift in Theology for me. This time it was my turn to be able to co-operate with a colleague in changing the way postgraduates and undergraduates were taught Christian doctrine. David Brown's appointment as Van Mildert Canon Professor in 1990 made possible a profound shift in the focus of his attention whilst sustaining his reputation in philosophical theology.[19] As it happened, I discovered he had been on the Scott Holland Trust committee which had invited me to give lectures on 'Theology and the Significance of Gender'.

A compulsory lecture course for some 80+ first year students, with the Apostles' Creed

[19] Major publications have followed in his case. A recent brief and accessible introduction to his perspective is David Brown, 'Supplying theology's missing link', *New Blackfriars*, 101:1092 (2020), 153-162; forthcoming: *Gospel as Work of Art: Imaginative Truth and the Open Text* (Grand Rapids:Eerdmans, 2022).

as the line of connection, required a move away from solely verbal delivery. Together, David Brown and I devised a lecture programme requiring attention to full-screen size 'artwork', something which would not have been possible before the advent of lecture theatres with up-to-date equipment, or indeed the determination to provide the slide collection required. Unsurprisingly, as well as students learning to 'read' the art-on-slides, this proved to be a sure-fire means to make it possible to engage the attention of those present, and to send them on searches for material on their own, given the 'prompts' of the study-packs of art and poetry and prose we provided to spur them on. The clue was to engage students' imagination without scriptural texts being in any way marginalised or disregarded. To the contrary: they required more attention rather than less.

Such an academic context apart, there are obviously significant practical and pastoral implications for this approach, in respect of questions about how people appropriate religious belief and the resources on which they draw, not least their own experiences. We also developed options unique in their time, on 'sacramentality and spirituality', for third year and MA levels, and involved musical examples as well (David Brown's familiarity with 'pop' was another asset). Then, for the general public, we ran a project on 'Sacramental Spirituality' which fed into a jointly organised series of occasions for the nine hundredth anniversary of the Cathedral (between October 1992 and December 1993). There were fourteen seminars and sixteen public lectures (with seven illustrated slide lectures) in the Cathedral itself.[20] One of the Cathedral occasions took the form of a poetry reading by a group of four of us, with music provided by some of the Choral Scholars of the

---

[20]   See eds. David Brown and Ann Loades, *The Sense of the Sacramental: Movement and Measure in Art and Music, Place and Time* (London: SPCK, 1995) with the introduction, 'The Dance of Grace', 1-16; and the same eds., *Christ the Sacramental Word: Incarnation Sacrament and Poetry* (London: SPCK, 1996), with the introduction. 'The Divine Poet', 1-25.

Cathedral, and a book of poetry from our best 'reader' developed from that occasion.[21] Then, for the University's contribution to the 'Year of the Visual Arts' in 1996, we ran a short series of five public lectures (with distinguished visitors) on 'Spirituality and the Visual Arts'. All in all, this has opened up a new area of Theology for me in my 'retirement' – with much gratitude to all those who continue to make it possible![22]

[21]   Eds. David Brown and David Fuller, *Signs of Grace: The Sacraments in Poetry and Prose* (London: Cassell, 1995).

[22]   e. g. 'Word and Sacrament' in ed. Stephen Burns and Ann Loades, *Grace and Glory in One Another's Faces. Preaching and Worship* (Norwich: Canterbury Press, 2020),100-115; 'Some straws in the wind: Reflections toward theological engagement with Theatre Dance' in ed. Christopher Brewer, *Christian Theology and the Transformation of Natural Religion* (Leuven/Paris/Bristol: Peeters, 2018) 191-205.

Ann Loades:
Curriculum Vitae

2009–   Honorary Professor, University of St Andrews.

2007–08   Lay Canon, Durham Cathedral; now Lay Canon Emerita 2008–.

2006–2020   Member of the Council/Academic Board of The Archbishop's Examination in Theology.

2005–06   President, Society for the Study of Theology 1 Jan 2005–31 Dec 2006.

2003   Emeritus Professor of Divinity, University of Durham.

2003–2011   Chair, Durham Cathedral Choir Association.

2001   CBE in New Year Honours List (after C. F. D. Moule, the second CBE for 'Services to Theology'). First woman Lay Member and one of two first Lay Members of Durham Cathedral Chapter, 2001–2007.

2003   Co-chair, Steering Committee, HEFCE Learning and Teaching Support Network, based at the University of Leeds and Lampeter, University of Wales: Philosophical and Religious Studies.

1999–2003   Panel Convener for Philosophy, Religious Studies and Law, Arts and Humanities Research Board. Member of the AHRB/C Postgraduate committee, and committee to decide on new Research Centres.

2000   Honorary Professorial Fellow, St Chad's College, Durham.

1995–2002   Member of Church of England Doctrine Commission.

1995   Professor of Divinity (personal chair; the first for a woman at Durham).

1991–1997   Editor of *Theology*.

1991   Visiting Research Fellow, Institute for Advanced Studies in the Humanities, Edinburgh University.

1990   Promoted to Reader.

1989–91	Chairwoman, Board of Studies in Theology, Durham University.
1988	Visiting Professor in Philosophy, Luther College, Decorah, Iowa (Fall semester).
1986	Visiting Professor in Religion, Rhodes College, Memphis (Easter term).
1983–85	Dean of the Faculty of Divinity, Durham University.
1981	Promoted to Senior Lecturer.
1975	Lecturer (full-time) Durham University.

Select Recent Writings

'Reforming Women in England and Scotland: Claiming Authority to Speak of God' in Kerrie Handasyde, Cathryn McKinney, Rebekah Pryor (eds), *Contemporary Feminist Theologies: Power, Authority, Love*. (Abingdon/New York: Routledge, 2021), pp. 100-116.

'Some Scottish Episcopal Theologians and the Arts.' *Scottish Episcopal Church Institute Journal 5*, 2 (Summer 2021) , 75-88.

'The Revelation of Abuse: Some Personal Reflections.' *Scottish Episcopal Church Institute Journal 5*, 1 (Spring 2021): 17-30.

Grace is Not Faceless: Reflections on Mary. Edited and introduced by Stephen Burns. London: Darton, Longman & Todd, 2021.

'Think about Cathedrals: Discover Ecclesiology,' *Modern Believing* vol. 61 (3), 2020: 251-258.

Grace and Glory in One Another's Faces: Preaching and Worship. Edited and introduced by Stephen Burns. Norwich: Canterbury Press, 2020.

Living the Story: The Ignatian Way of Prayer. Edited on behalf of Joseph Cassidy. Norwich: Canterbury Press, 2020.

'A wake-up call?' *Theology* vol.123 (2), 2020: 124-128.

'Evelyn Underhill (1875-1941): Mysticism in Fiction' in Judith Maltby and Alison Shell (eds.), *Anglican Women Novelists* (London/New York: T&T Clark/Bloomsbury 2019), pp.73-84, 227-231.

'More Catholic than Rome; more reformed than Geneva: Joseph P. Cassidy and possibilities for renewal in the Church of England', *International Journal for the Study of the Christian Church*, 19:1 (2018): 1-13.

'Lazarus without limits: scripture, tradition and the cultural life of a text', *International Journal for the Study of the Christian Church*, vol. 18, no. 2-3 (2018 special issue, 'Reflecting a Catholic

Mind' in memory of Bishop Geoffrey Rowell), 252-264.

'Some Straws in the Wind: Reflections towards theological engagement with Theatre Dance' in Christopher R. Brewer (ed.), *Christian Theology and the Transformation of Natural Religion: Essays in Honour of David Brown* (Leuven: Peeters 2018), 191-205.

'L'impatto della Riforma in Inghilterra e Scozia' in Letizia Tomassone e Adriana Valerio (eds.), *Bibbia, donne, profezia. A partire dalla Riforma*, Firenze: Nerbini, 2018, 57-69. Italian translation of a paper given at a conference organised by the Coordinamento Teologie Italiane and the Faculta Valdese di Teologia di Roma, 2017.

'A Priestly Role for Music: Concluding Reflection' in Michael O'Connor, Hyun-Ah Kim and Christina Labriola (eds.), *Music, Theology, and Justice* (Lexington Books 2017), 211-216.

'Anglican Spirituality' in M. Chapman, S. Clarke and M.Percy (eds.), *The Oxford Handbook of Anglican Studies*, OUP, 2015), 149-164.

'**Simone Weil**' in C. Meister and J.Beilby (eds.), *The Routledge Companion to Modern Christian Thought* (Routledge, 2013), 207-216.

'**Mysticism: The Energetic Love**' in L. Nestrop and S. Podmore (eds.), *Exploring Lost Dimensions in Christian Mysticism* (Ashgate 2013), 117-129.

'**Dorothy L. Sayers: War and Redemption**' in E. Henderson and D. Hein (eds.), *C.S. Lewis and Friends: Faith and the Power of the Imagination* (SPCK, 2011), 53-70.

'**Introduction**' in each of the Wipf & Stock republication of *The Sacred Plays of Dorothy L. Sayers* (2011), 7-20 or equivalent.

'**Elizabeth Cady Standon's The Woman's Bible**', in M. Lieb, E. Mason and J. Roberts (eds.), *The Oxford Handbook of the Reception History of the Bible* (OUP, 2011), 307-322.

'**Evelyn Underhill (1895-1941): Mysticism and Worship**', *International Journal for the Study of the Christian Church* 10:1 (2010), 57-70.

'Simone Weil: Resistance and Writing', *International Journal of Public Theology* 4:1 (2010), 100-117.

'On Gender' in R.C. MacSwain and M.Ward (eds.),*Cambridge Companion to C.S. Lewis* (Cambridge, 2010), 16-173.